Navigation For Pilots

Simplified

Captain John Swan

POOLEYS FLIGHT EQUIPMENT

Copyright 2007 © Pooleys Flight Equipment Ltd
Navigation for Pilots Simplified - John Swan

ISBN: 978-1-84336-134-3

Published by:
Pooleys Flight Equipment Ltd
Elstree Aerodrome
Elstree
Hertfordshire WD6 3AW

Tel: +44(0)20 8953 4870
Fax: +44(0)20 8953 2512
Email: sales@pooleys.com
Website: www.pooleys.com

Third Edition 2007
Second Edition 2002
First Edition 1997

Contents

Navigation Section

Radio Navigation Section

Navigation Section

1

Form of the Earth.

For navigational purposes the earth is considered to be a sphere, in actual fact the diameter at the poles is smaller than at the equator.

Axis and Poles.

The earth rotates about an axis passing through the true North and South poles in an easterly direction. The points on the earth's surface an equal distance from each pole form a circular line called the equator. The magnetic poles used for navigation are not coincident with the axis of rotation.

Meridians of Longitude.

Meridians of longitude are lines on the surface of the earth directly linking the true North and South poles that cross the equator at right angles. The angular position of these meridians are referenced to the prime meridian passing through Greenwich in England, being from 0⁰ to 180⁰ either East or West of it.

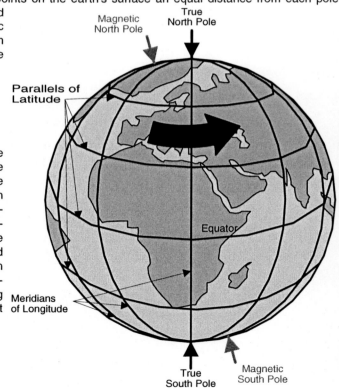

Magnetic North Pole

True North Pole

Parallels of Latitude

Equator

Meridians of Longitude

True South Pole

Magnetic South Pole

1

Parallels of Latitude.

Parallels of latitude are circles on the surface of the earth parallel to the equator, they also cut the meridians at right angles. These parallels of latitude are referenced by their angular position above or below the equator, those above being from 0^0 to 90^0 North and those below being from 0^0 to 90^0 South.

To allow the angular position of a point to be more accurately defined the degree (^{0}) is divided into 60 minutes (') which itself is further divided into 60 seconds("). This applies to both meridians of longitude and parallels of latitude.

Great Circles, Small Circles and Rhumb Lines.

Great Circle.

A great circle is a circle on the earth's surface whose centre and radius are that of the earth. Routing along a great circle is the shortest distance between two points, for long routes the aircraft's heading will be continually changing to follow this route.

The equator is a great circle and meridians of longitude are semi-great circles.

Small Circle.

A small circle is a circle on the earth's surface whose radius and centre are not that of the earth. Parallels of latitude, except the equator, are small circles.

Rhumb Lines.

A rhumb line is any line on the earth's surface that crosses all meridians at a constant angle. An aircraft flying a constant heading is following a rhumb line. Parallels of latitude and meridians of longitude are all rhumb lines.

Hemispheres, North/South and East/West.

Hemispheres describe the splitting of the earth into two halves. If the equator is used as the split then we have a Northern and Southern hemisphere, whereas if the prime meridian is used we have an Eastern and Western hemisphere.

2

Mapping.

Aeronautical Maps and Charts (Topographical).

The term map originates from the mapping of land masses and the term chart originates from the charting of sea areas, now either term is used for land or sea. Topographical refers to the nature of the earth's surface and is portrayed on the map or chart to enable the pilot to navigate by reference to these features.

Projections and their Properties.

The two most common projections used for aviation charts are the Lambert Conformal Conic projection and the Mercator projection. The former is used by most States for VFR aeronautical charts whereas the latter is only used on charts covering equatorial regions, or in non-equatorial regions for small areas due to the scale varying significantly with latitude. The UK use transverse Mercator charts for their 1:250,000 series aeronautical charts.

Irrespective of what projection is used the chart must have certain properties to allow it to project the earth's surface accurately enough to be used for navigation.

Conformality.

Conformality means the angle between points on the earth's surface is shown accurately on the chart. This is the most important property.

Equivalence.

Equivalence means the shape of features on the earth's surface are shown accurately on the chart, This is not a prime requirement provided the shapes are not too distorted.

Scale.

The scale of a chart is the ratio of chart length divided by earth distance. The scale of the chart should be constant over the whole chart. This is not a prime requirement provided for practical purposes it appears constant.

Great Circles and Rhumb Lines.

For navigation purposes it is desirable that both of these appear as straight lines on the chart, obviously on charts covering a large area this will not be possible.

Conformal Conic Projection.

Main Properties.

The Lambert Conformal Conic projection has the following properties:

The chart is conformal.

The chart has equivalence, areas are accurately portrayed.

The chart scale varies slightly but for practical purposes it appears constant.

The chart depicts great circles as straight lines, rhumb lines are depicted as curves being concave to the nearest pole, but meridians of longitude are depicted as straight lines.

Construction.

The chart is constructed by wrapping the chart around the earth so that it cuts the surface at the two standard parallels of latitude. This will result in a cone being formed with the surface details of the selected area being indented into the chart.

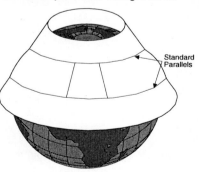

Standard Parallels

Convergence of Meridians.

When the cone is opened up the meridians of longitude will converge towards the nearest pole.

Presentation of Meridians, Parallels, Great Circles and Rhumb Lines.

The meridians of longitude will be depicted as straight lines converging towards the nearest pole.

The parallels of latitude will be depicted as curved lines concave to the nearest pole.

Great circles will be depicted as straight lines.

Rhumb lines will be depicted as curved lines concave to the nearest pole, with the exception of meridians which are depicted as straight lines.

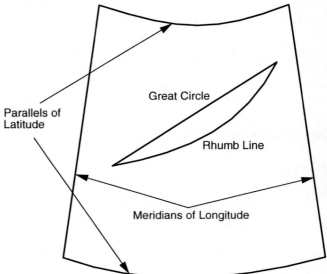

Scale and Standard Parallels.

Meridians of longitude and parallels of latitude are shown on the chart in one degree increments but depending upon the scale of the chart these may have additional markings indicating minutes or multiples of minutes.

The nautical mile is the most commonly used distance measurement in aviation and by definition is 1 minute of latitude. The meridians of longitude shown on the chart have a latitude scale superimposed on them marked in minutes, or multiples, that can be used to indicate nautical miles.

Note, due to the parallels of latitude being small circles the longitude scale superimposed on them can not be used to represent nautical miles directly.

Standard parallels are the parallels of latitude used to construct the chart, they also form the extremities of the chart.

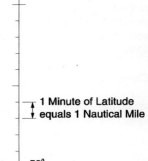

Depiction of Height.

Height can be depicted on a chart in many ways:

Colour Coding.

By using colour, areas of different height easily stand out. The normal convention is to depict low ground as white and high ground as dark brown, areas in between are depicted in various shades of yellow and brown.

Written Numbers.

Points of known height are written on the chart, these may be spot heights or tall man-made structures.

Contour Lines.

These are lines on the chart linking points of equal height together. By comparing the closeness of the contours the steepness of a hill or mountain can be assessed.

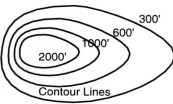

Cross section of above

Hachuring.

Short lines radiating from high ground.

Hill Shading.

Shading gives the impression of shadows formed by hills at sunrise or sunset.

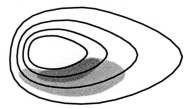

3

Direction.

Direction can refer to where the aircraft is going or where it is pointing, the former is the aircraft's ground track and the latter is its heading. Also these ground tracks and headings can be referenced to true, magnetic or compass North.

True North.

True North is the direction from any point on the earth that would take an aircraft directly to the North pole, this being the North pole about which the earth rotates. When measuring the direction for a flight from a chart the reference used is true North.

The Earth's Magnetic Field.

The earth's magnetic field describes the flow of magnetism from one of the earth's magnetic poles to the other.

Variation.

The earth rotates about the true North and South pole, but magnetic North and South are not coincident with the poles about which the earth rotates. This leads to the magnetic poles being offset from the true poles by a varying amount depending upon the observer's position on the earth. In addition the earth's magnetic field is not uniform, it is affected by local magnetic disturbances within the earth's core which will attract the magnet in the compass. These two effects are referred to as magnetic variation and are shown on aeronautical maps as isogonal lines linking points of equal magnetic variation.

In simple terms magnetic variation is the magnetic heading indicated when pointing at true North.

Annual Change.

Due to changes occurring in the earth's core the variation will change with time, reference to an aeronautical chart will show the predicted annual variation.

Magnetic North.

Magnetic North is the direction the needle of a magnetic compass will point and is the directional reference used by an aircraft in flight. The magnetic heading an aircraft is required to fly is calculated from its true heading by adding or subtracting the variation, Westerly variations are added whereas Easterly are subtracted.

When going from true to magnetic this can be remembered by:

West is **B**est, <u>East</u> is <u>Least</u>.

Vertical and Horizontal Components.

The direction of this magnetic flow will be affected by its position on the earth, at the poles it will be vertical and at the equator it will be horizontal. The horizontal component of the flow is the one indicating the direction of the magnetic pole and this is the one the magnet in the compass is required to follow to indicate the aircraft's heading. The vertical component will cause the magnet in the compass to point down towards the ground, the effect increasing with increasing latitude. This deflection downwards from the horizontal is called dip angle and the magnetic compass utilises a pendulous mass hung below the magnet to reduce this dip angle.

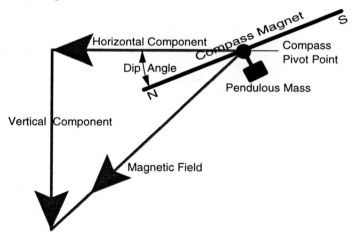

Isogonals and Agonic Lines.

Isogonals are lines on charts of equal variation and an agonic line shows where there is no variation. In this case true North and magnetic North are in line.

4

Aircraft Magnetism.

Magnetic Influences within the Aircraft.

The magnet in the compass is attracted by any magnetic source, not only the earth's magnet field but by ferrous materials and electrical sources within the aircraft.

Compass Deviation.

FOR	STEER
N	01
30	29
60	60
E	91
120	118
150	148
S	181
210	210
240	240
W	W
300	301
330	329

RADIO ON
20.11.96
G-ZXXZ

The effect of magnetism from the aircraft on the reading of the compass is referred to as deviation, this deviation is likely to vary with different headings so the aircraft is fitted with a deviation card. This deviation card is calibrated by doing a compass swing where the aircraft's compass readings are compared with an external reference compass, the card indicates the deviation at 30⁰ intervals.

Compass heading is converted from magnetic heading by adding or subtracting the deviation, Westerly deviations are added and Easterly are subtracted.

When going from magnetic to compass this can be remembered by:

West is Best, East is Least.

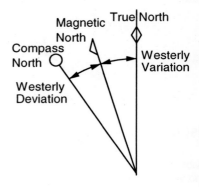

9

Avoiding Magnetic Interference of the Compass.

The pilot must take care not to place any magnetic material near the compass since this is the pilot's primary heading reference. Magnetic goods can include things as harmless as a metallic pen or screw driver, even the installation of a GPS in the vicinity of the compass will require it to be swung again.

Turning and Acceleration Errors.

The compass has inherent errors that are noticeable when the aircraft is either turning or accelerating and decelerating. In both cases these errors are due to the pendulous weight fitted to the compass to compensate for dip angle.

Magnetic dip causes the pendulous weight's centre of gravity not to be vertically below the pivot point.

Turning errors occur due to the pivot point being pulled into the turn whereas the pendulous weight is thrown out from the turn by centrifugal force. This effect is most noticeable when turning through North or South and is not present when turning through East or West. In the northern hemisphere when entering a turn from a heading of North the compass will initially indicate a turn in the opposite direction. When rolling out onto a heading of North the pilot must roll out prior to the compass indicating North, the amount of lead is approximately half the helicopter's latitude. When entering a turn from a heading of South the compass will initially indicate a higher rate of turn than is actually occurring, when rolling out onto a heading of South the pilot must overshoot South by approximately half the aircraft's latitude.

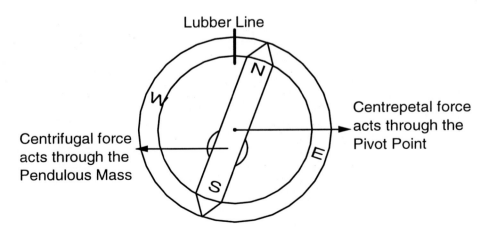

Lubber Line

Centrepetal force acts through the Pivot Point

Centrifugal force acts through the Pendulous Mass

Acceleration and deceleration errors are a maximum on headings of East and West and are not present on headings of North or South. When the aircraft accelerates the pivot point is pulled forward but the pendulous weight is left behind. Since the magnet is across the aircraft this will cause the compass card to rotate and indicate a turn towards North. Similarly a deceleration will have the opposite effect indicating a turn towards South.

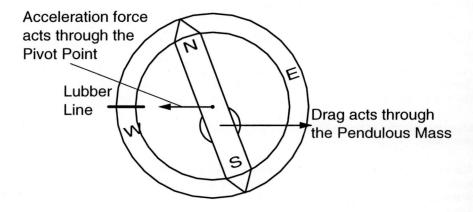

5

Distances.

Units.

The two standards adopted by the aviation industry for measuring distance are the nautical mile and the kilometre.

The nautical mile is defined as the distance on the earth's surface for a one minute change in latitude.

The kilometre is defined as the average distance from the poles to the equator divided by 10,000.

Conversion of Units.

The nautical mile and the kilometre are the most common units of distance used in aviation, both of these are based on the average distance from the poles to the equator.

One nautical mile equals one minute of latitude, there are 60 minutes in a degree, and the distance from the poles to the equator is 90 degrees. Therefore the distance from the poles to the equator equals 1 x 60 x 90 = 5,400 nautical miles.

The kilometre is defined as the distance from the poles to the equator divided by 10,000.

Therefore 5,400 nautical miles equals 10,000 kilometres.

1 nautical mile equals 1.852 kilometres.

1 kilometre equals 0.54 nautical miles.

Heights are depicted in either feet or metres.

1 foot equals 0.3048 metres.

1 metre equals 3.2808 feet.

Measurement of Distance in Relationship to Map Projection.

When measuring distance on a Conformal Conic or Transverse Mercator chart either a scale rule or dividers can be used.

If the chart is a Mercator care must be taken when using dividers to use the scale relevant to the latitude of the flight.

6

Charts in Practical Navigation.

Plotting Positions.

Positions are plotted on a chart by reference to:

Features on the earth.

Latitude and longitude.

Navigation aids.

Latitude and Longitude.

Latitude and longitude form a grid covering the whole surface of the earth which can be used to specify position.

A latitude and longitude co-ordinate specifies the latitude of the position either North or South of the equator and the longitude either East or West of the prime meridian.

For example:

52⁰ 15' 30" N, 006⁰ 30' 20" W

This position is 52 degrees 15 minutes 30 seconds North of the equator and 6 degrees 30 minutes 20 seconds West of the prime meridian.

To plot this position on a chart:

Locate the intersection of the 52 degree parallel with the 6 degree meridian.

Using the scale on the meridian move up 15 minutes 30 seconds and mark it.

Locate the intersection of the 52 degree parallel with 7 degree meridian.

Using the scale on the meridian move up 15 minutes 30 seconds and mark it.

Draw a line linking these two marked points, this is the 52⁰ 15' 30" North parallel.

Using the scale on the 52 degree parallel move westwards to 006⁰ 30' 20" West and mark it.

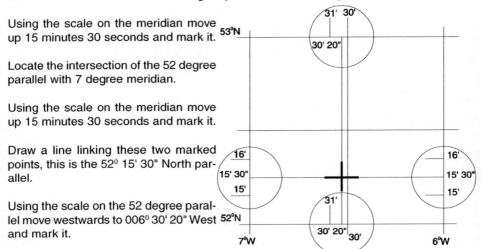

Using the scale on the 52 degree 30 minute, or 53 degree parallel move westwards to 006⁰ 30' 20" West and mark it.

Draw a line linking these two marked points, this is the 006⁰ 30' 20" West meridian.

The intersection of the two lines is our point 52⁰ 15' 30" N, 006⁰ 30' 20" W.

The accuracy of the plot depends upon the scale of the chart and whether the co-ordinates given are to the nearest minute or second. Remember one minute of latitude is one nautical mile, a nautical mile is approximately two kilometres, it is actually 1.852 km, therefore one second of latitude is approximately 30 metres.

Bearing and Distance.

An alternative method of defining a position is its distance and bearing from a known point, this point may be a prominent feature or a radio navigation aid. In either case the position is plotted in the same manner by:

Locate the known point.

Draw a line from that point in the direction given.

With a compass or ruler mark off the distance from the known point to give the position.

Use of the Navigation Protractor.

The navigation protractor is a 360° protractor used for plotting or measuring bearings on an aeronautical chart. The protractor is square and has a rectangular grid to allow it to be easily aligned with the meridians of longitude on a chart. Angles are measured by placing the protractor with its centre midway along the line plotted on the chart. The arrow on the protractor should be pointing approximately to North, this is accurately aligned by slightly rotating the protractor so the vertical lines of the grid are parallel to one of the meridians. The angle the line makes with reference to true North is read off where it crosses the edge of the protractor.

When measuring bearings from a point place the centre of the protractor over the point and read off the bearing where the line crosses the edge of the protractor.

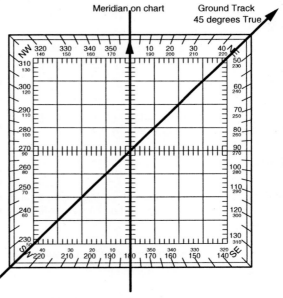

Measurement of Tracks and Distances.

Tracks refer to the direction of the lines plotted on a chart and are measured using the navigation protractor, distances are measured using either dividers or a ruler.

Tracks are measured by placing the centre of the navigation protractor midway along the plotted line. The arrow on the protractor should be pointing approximately to North, this is accurately aligned by slightly rotating the protractor so the vertical lines of the grid are parallel to one of the meridians. The track the line makes with reference to true North is read off where it crosses the edge of the protractor.

Since a plotted line can be flown either from A to B, or from B to A the protractor will give two angles, 180 degrees apart. To avoid confusion assume the aircraft is at the centre of the protractor and move along the plotted line in the direction of intended flight and read off the track.

Distances can be measured either by using a scaled ruler marked in nautical miles or kilometres, or by using dividers and reading off the gap distance from the scale on the edge of the chart.

7

Chart Reference Information.

Topography.

Topography refers to the nature of the earth's surface and is portrayed on the map or chart to enable the pilot to navigate by reference to these features.

Relief.

Relief refers to the variation of height across a land mass. A chart without any means of showing hills and valleys would make navigation by visual references difficult and dangerous. Relief is shown on charts by the use of:

Contour lines, these link points of equal height together. The closeness of the contour lines gives a direct indication of the steepness of the terrain.

Colour, low land is depicted by white and high ground by dark brown. The rate of colour change indicating the steepness of the terrain.

Hachuring, short lines radiating from high ground.

Hill Shading gives the impression of shadows formed by hills at sunrise or sunset.

Cultural Features.

Cultural features are portrayed on the map or chart to allow the pilot to navigate by reference to these features.

Note, States may use alternative symbols on their aeronautical charts, refer to the legend at the bottom of the chart or the AIP.

These symbols are portrayed on the UK 1:500,000 aeronautical charts as follows:

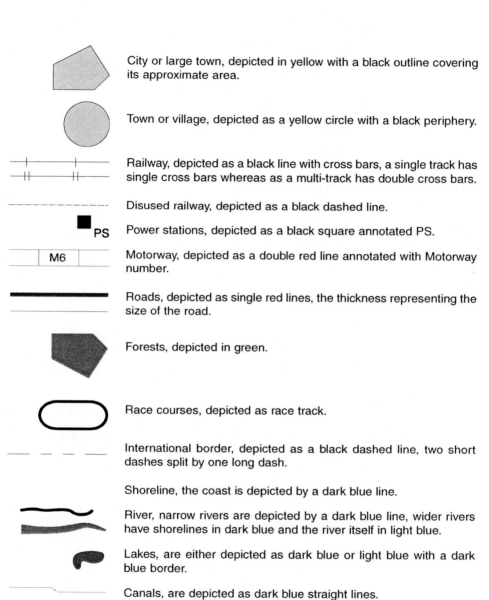

City or large town, depicted in yellow with a black outline covering its approximate area.

Town or village, depicted as a yellow circle with a black periphery.

Railway, depicted as a black line with cross bars, a single track has single cross bars whereas as a multi-track has double cross bars.

Disused railway, depicted as a black dashed line.

Power stations, depicted as a black square annotated PS.

Motorway, depicted as a double red line annotated with Motorway number.

Roads, depicted as single red lines, the thickness representing the size of the road.

Forests, depicted in green.

Race courses, depicted as race track.

International border, depicted as a black dashed line, two short dashes split by one long dash.

Shoreline, the coast is depicted by a dark blue line.

River, narrow rivers are depicted by a dark blue line, wider rivers have shorelines in dark blue and the river itself in light blue.

Lakes, are either depicted as dark blue or light blue with a dark blue border.

Canals, are depicted as dark blue straight lines.

Contours are depicted as brown lines with the elevation in feet imposed upon them.

3559. Maximum Chart Elevation, indicated by a dot, elevation printed in bold black surrounded by a black box.

.**1434** Spot heights, indicated by a dot, elevation printed in black.

Aeronautical Symbols.

Aeronautical symbols are the symbols on the chart depicting features on the ground of interest to pilots, these include aerodromes and obstructions.

Note, States may use alternative symbols on their aeronautical charts, refer to the legend at the bottom of the chart or the AIP.

These symbols are portrayed on the UK 1:500,000 aeronautical charts as follows:

Civil Aerodrome, depicted by a red circle with short ticks on the four cardinal headings.

Civil Aerodrome with no facilities, depicted by a red circle.

Civil Heliport, depicted by a red circle with a H in it.

Military Aerodrome available for civil use, depicted by a double blue concentric circle with ticks on the four cardinal headings.

Military Aerodrome, depicted by a double blue concentric circle.

Military Heliport, depicted by a double blue concentric circle with a H in it.

Disused Aerodrome, depicted by a blue or red circle with a cross in it.

150   Aerodrome Elevation in feet AMSL written under the aerodrome name.

Manchester   Customs Aerodrome, depicted by the aerodrome name being surrounded by a red dashed box.

☆ FIG ⦂⎯⎯⦂
☆ FIR ⦂⎯⦂⦂   Aerodrome Light Beacon.

Ⓜ   Intensive Microlight Activity, depicted as a red circle with a M in it.

(G) cables Glider Launching Site, depicted in red or blue, primary activity depicted as a G in a circle or if additional activities then a double cross in a rectangle.

┌─┼─┼─┐ cables Cables indicates launch cables up to 2000 feet AGL.

Aerodrome Traffic Zone (ATZ) indicates regulated airspace around an aerodrome up to 2000 feet above aerodrome elevation, radius 2 nm for runways up to 1850m or 2.5 nm for runways greater than 1850m, depicted as a blue shaded circle.

 Free Fall Parachuting Site, depicted as a red or blue circle with a parachute symbol in it.

Hang or Para Gliding Activity, wings depicted in red alone indicates foot launch.

cables ◄►cables
Primary   Additional
Activity   Activity

Wings and cables or rectangle with solid triangle in it indicates winch launching, cables may go up to 3,000 feet AGL.

Single   Multiple

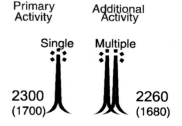

2300   2260
(1700)   (1680)

Exceptionally High Obstacle (lighted), above 1,000 feet, depicted in blue, single, multiple.

850 /\   805 /\/\
(350) /.\   (310) /\/\

Obstacles (unlighted), depicted in blue, single, multiple.

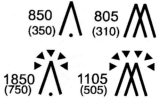

1850 /\   1105 /\/\
(750) /.\   (505) /\/\

Obstacles (lighted), depicted in blue, single, multiple.

∿∿∿∿∿∿∿ cables   Cables joining obstacles are depicted in blue.

Only known obstacles above 300 feet AGL are shown.

. Fl(2)30.0secs   Marine light, depicted as a red dot with abbreviation of the lights colour and frequency of transmission.

⊥ FIWR 15.0secs   Lightship, depicted as a red ship with abbreviation of the lights colour and frequency of transmission.

Maximum Elevation Figures (MEF) show the highest known elevation for each quadrangle taking into account terrain, obstacles and allowing for unknown features. These are not SAFETY HEIGHTS.

Aeronautical Information.

Aeronautical information is overlaid on the map or chart to show areas of controlled and restricted airspace, and the location of navigation aids and reporting points.

Note, States may use alternative symbols on their aeronautical charts, refer to the legend at the bottom of the chart or the AIP.

This information is portrayed on the UK 1:500,000 aeronautical charts as follows:

⊙ Basic Radio Facility, depicted by a blue circle with a dot in the middle.

NDB, depicted by a blue circle with a dot in the middle surrounded by a circle of small blue dots.

 VOR, depicted by a blue compass rose with a small hexagon in the middle.

DME, depicted by a blue square with a dot in the middle.

Co-Located VOR and DME, depicted by a blue square bordering a blue hexagon with a dot in the middle.

TACAN, depicted as a blue sort of square cornered triangle with a dot in the middle.

Class of airspace is indicated by the appropriate letter in a blue square.

R41 A FL35+

Controlled airspace is shown with a blue tint.

Flight Information Region boundaries, a blue line with ticks on alternate sides.

BELFAST CTR SFC-FL105   Control Area (CTA) and Control Zone boundaries, a dashed blue line.

750'-2000'   Low Level Corridors or Special Routes are blue tinted with dashed blue lines indicating the borders.

Radar Advisory Service Zone or Area boundary, alternating blue dots and dashes.

21

Special Access Lane Entry/Exit shown by a blue arrow.

Visual Reporting Point (VRP) depicted by a blue circle with a blue cross in it.

Airway, bordered by a blue line, the airway name and its vertical dimensions printed within the airway.

Advisory Route, a dashed blue line with the route's name superimposed on it.

▲ Compulsory Reporting Point, depicted by a solid blue triangle.

△ On Request Reporting Point, depicted by a white triangle with blue border.

Military Aerodrome Traffic Zones (MATZs) are depicted by a circle of blue dots filled with a red tint, with a diameter of 5 nm with stubs aligned with the runways, these being 5 nm long and 4 nm wide. Vertically the circle is from the ground up to 3,000 feet AAL and the stubs from 1,000 feet AAL up to 3,000 feet AAL. The MATZ penetration frequency is annotated in the circle, if the abbreviation LARS is also present it indicates this aerodrome offers the Lower Airspace Radar Service

Isogonals, depicted as blue dashed lines indicating the variation and date it was measured, the chart legend should indicate the yearly change.

Permanent

By NOTAM

Airspace Restrictions are bordered in red, with shading on the inside of the boundary. Those areas that are activated by notam have a dashed border. The types of area are indicated by D Danger, P Prohibited and R Restricted, followed by its reference number and after the / its altitude limit in thousands of feet AMSL. Weapon Range Danger Areas (WRDAs) may have military aircraft operating outside these areas, civilian pilots operating in the vicinity of WRDAs should use the associated Radar Service. A Danger Area crossing service is indicated by a † prefixing the reference number.

Areas of Intense Aerial Activity (AIAA) are border by a red tint, they are annotated by name giving the operating altitudes and the controlling authority and frequency.

High Intensity Radio Transmission Areas (HIRTA) are depicted as a red circle of 0.5 nm radius tinted in red, they are annotated with their effective altitude in thousands of feet AMSL.

Bird Sanctuaries are depicted as a red circle with a bird in it, they are annotated by a name and effective altitude in thousands of feet AMSL.

Gas Venting Operations (GVSs) are depicted as a red circle, they are annotated by GVS/ followed by its effective altitude in thousands of feet AMSL.

GVS/3.1

Altimeter Setting Regions (ASRs) are bordered by a series of red double crosses.

8

Principles of Navigation.

IAS, RAS (CAS) and TAS.

These are all abbreviations for airspeeds.

IAS.

Indicated airspeed is the airspeed shown on the aircraft's airspeed indicator.

RAS, CAS.

Rectified airspeed or calibrated airspeed is the airspeed shown on the airspeed indicator corrected for both instrument and position error.

TAS.

True airspeed is the rectified airspeed corrected for pressure, altitude and temperature.

Track, True and Magnetic.

Track is the direction of the line plotted on the chart, hence it is also the direction the aircraft is to fly across the ground.

This track may be either referenced to true North, as in the initial plotting stage, or magnetic North once the aircraft gets airborne.

Wind Velocity, Heading and Ground Speed.

Wind velocity describes the direction from which the wind is coming and its speed. Upper winds received from the meteorological office are referenced to true North, these are used for flight planning. To confuse matters, surface winds reported by the tower are referenced to magnetic North.

Heading describes the direction the nose of the aircraft is pointing, it may be referenced to true, magnetic or compass North. In the flight planning stage it is referenced to true North then prior to flight it is converted to a magnetic or compass heading.

The aircraft is flying with reference to the air around it, not the ground, therefore if there is a wind the aircraft is likely to be blown off course. This is analogous to trying to swim across a river, you get swept downstream.

This wind may not only blow the aircraft off course but it may speed it up, if there is a tail wind component, or slow it down if there is a head wind component. Therefore the ground speed of the aircraft is not only affected by its true airspeed but also by the wind.

Triangle of Velocities.

The triangle of velocities allows the pilot to calculate the ground speed and the required heading to fly to compensate for the forecast wind.

A triangle consists of three interconnected sides, each of these sides represents a velocity, it has direction and speed (length).

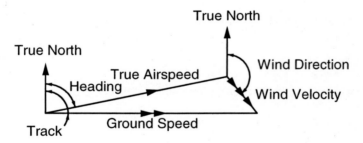

One side represents the wind, if in a balloon you would be blown along this side of the triangle.

The second side represents the heading and true airspeed of the aircraft, this is the direction and distance the aircraft would fly in no wind conditions.

The third side is the combined effect of the first two and is the ground track and ground speed of the aircraft.

Calculation of Heading and Ground Speed.

At the flight planning stage the pilot has the following information:

True airspeed.

Ground track.

Wind direction and speed.

The following information is unknown:

Heading.

Ground Speed.

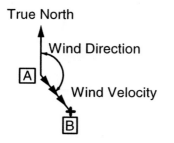

With four of the six variables known it is possible to construct a triangle of velocities.

The wind is drawn, from say A to B, the direction being with reference to true North and the length being equal to the wind speed.

From A the ground track is drawn, the direction being with reference to true North but the ground speed is unknown so the length of the line is also unknown.

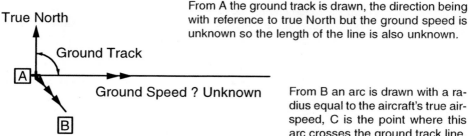

From B an arc is drawn with a radius equal to the aircraft's true airspeed, C is the point where this arc crosses the ground track line.

A straight line is drawn from B to C, the angle this line makes to true North is the aircraft's required heading.

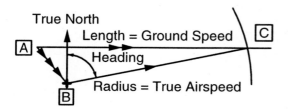

The length of the ground track line from A to C is the ground speed.

Drift and Wind Correction Angle.

Drift is the angle between the heading flown and the ground track resulting from that heading.

The wind correction angle is the angle between the ground track and the required heading to maintain that ground track. Drift and wind correction angle are of the same magnitude but one is to the left and the other to the right.

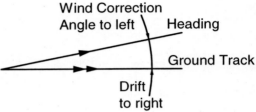

ETA.

This is the estimated time of arrival and is found by dividing the ground track distance by the ground speed, a small addition may be added for the climb out and approach phases.

Dead Reckoning, Position and Fix.

Dead reckoning is a form of navigation where the pilot estimates his position by reference to his flight planned ground speed and ground track.

A fix is a confirmed position, this may be a feature familiar to the pilot or a unique feature found both on the earth's surface and on the chart. Following a fix the pilot can continue dead reckoning navigation but now the starting point for the next phase of flight is the fix.

The winds aloft are not always as forecast so the pilot following a fix may amend the heading and ground speed to follow more accurately the planned route.

9

The Navigation Computer.

The navigation computer discussed here is not an electronic device but a clever mechanical device having a wind computer on one side and a circular slide rule on the other for calculations and for converting units. The use of the Pooleys CRP-1 is described below. In principle the methods discussed are applicable to other manufacturer's computers, however reference should be made to their operating manuals.

Use of the Circular Slide Rule.

The circular slide rule side of the computer has two concentric circular scales, each scale having various abbreviations written around it in black, red and blue.

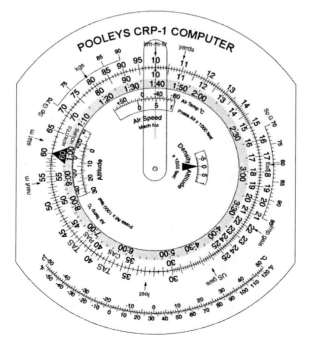

TAS, Time and Distance.

TAS, true airspeed is the rectified airspeed corrected for pressure altitude and temperature, rectified airspeed is found by using the table in the aircraft's flight manual to correct the indicated airspeed.

To calculate TAS:

Align the inner and outer scales, by rotating the inner scale so the two blue 10's are in line.

Referring to the Airspeed/Mach. No. window directly above the centre.

By gently rotating the moving scale set the outside air temperature, above the window against the pressure altitude, within the window.

Referring to the two concentric circular scales.

Locate the RAS on the inner scale and read off the value it corresponds to on the outer scale, this is the aircraft's TAS.

Example.

RAS	100 knots.
Pressure altitude	1,000 feet.
Outside air temperature	+25 °C.

1   Align two blue 10's.

2   Set +25 above the airspeed window against 1 within the window.

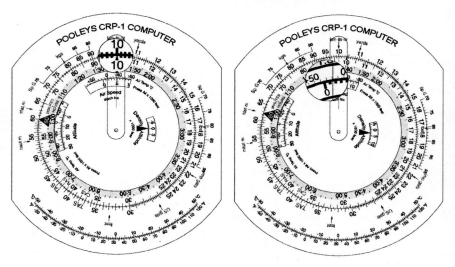

29

3 100 does not appear on the inner circular scale so divide by 10, 10 does appear on the scale and it corresponds to 10.35 on the outer, multiply by 10 to give a TAS of 103.5 knots.

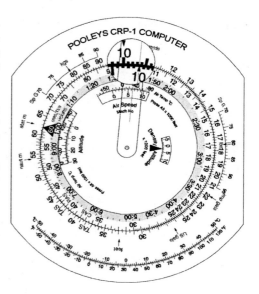

Note, the scales on the concentric circles go from 10 to 99, this means any number falling outside this range is catered for by moving the decimal point to the right or left. For example 1.5 would be treated as 15 as would 150 or 1,500. Care must be taken when finishing any calculation to ensure the decimal place is returned to its correct position. This is normally achieved by doing an approximation mentally, this will indicate the position of the decimal point.

To calculate velocity, time and distance.

Let us consider the relationships between velocity, distance and time.

Velocity = Distance / Time.

Distance = Velocity x Time.

Time = Distance / Velocity.

Some simple mental arithmetic will confirm these.

Driving a car at 50 mph for 2 hours will cover 100 miles, 50 x 2 = 100.

If only 60 miles was covered in the 2 hours then the speed was only 30 mph, 60 / 2 = 30.

If the original 100 miles was driven at 25 mph it would take 4 hours, 100 / 25 = 4.

Velocity, in our context is usually ground speed and is equal to the ground distance covered divided by the time it takes.

For all time and distance calculations the inner rotating circular scale represents time. Units of minutes use the black on white numbers whereas units of hours use the numbers in the yellow circular band. Velocity and distance are always represented on the outer scale.

To calculate velocity.

Rotate the inner scale to align the time taken, on the inner scale, with the distance covered on the outer scale.

Against the 60 in the black triangle read off the velocity on the outer scale.

Example.

Time   2 hours.

Distance   200 nm.

1   Locate 2.00 in the yellow band, this corresponds to 120 minutes, which is represented by 12.

2   Rotate the 12 to correspond with the 20, (200 divided by 10), on the outer scale.

3   Against the black triangle read off 10, giving the velocity as 100 knots, (10 x 10).

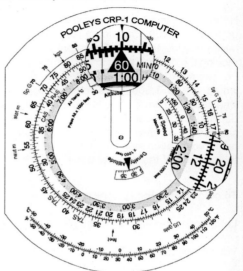

To calculate time.

Rotate the inner scale to line up the 60 in the black triangle with the aircraft's velocity on the outer scale.

Against the distance covered on the outer scale read off the time taken on the inner scale.

Example.

Velocity   120 knots.

Distance   240 nm.

1   Align the black triangle with 12, (120 divided by 10), on the outer scale.

2   Against 24, (240 divided by 10), on the outer scale read off the time as 2.00 hours or 120 minutes.

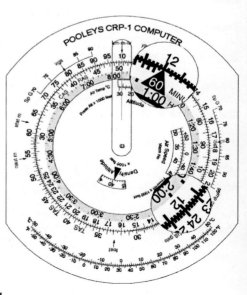

To calculate distance.

Rotate the inner scale to line up the 60 in the black triangle with the aircraft's velocity on the outer scale.

Against the time taken on the inner scale read off the distance covered on the outer scale.

Example.

Velocity   60 knots.

Time   3 hours.

1   Align the black triangle with 60 on the outer scale.

2   Against 3.00 on the inner yellow scale read off distance covered on outer scale as 180 nm, (18 x 10).

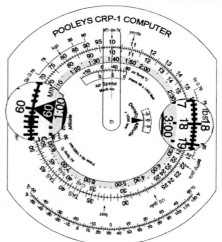

Conversion of Units.

Around the outer scale various units are printed in red, i.e. US gals, imp. gals etc., these are used to convert from one unit of measurement to another.

To convert a known quantity to an alternative unit of measurement line up the quantity on the inner scale against the known unit of measurement around the outer scale and against the required unit of measurement read off the quantity on the inner scale.

Example.

Convert 30 US gals to imp. gals and litres.

1   Line up 30 on the inner scale with US gals, just clockwise of 25 on the outer scale.

2   Against imp. gals, above 22 on outer scale, read off quantity of approximately 25 imp. gals on inner scale.

3   Against ltr, above 10 on outer scale, read off quantity of 113 litres on inner scale.

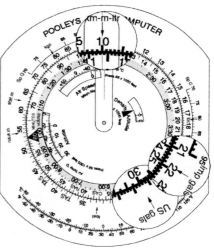

Note, to align the inner scale accurately with the arrows next to the units use the red rotary cursor.

Fuel Required.

The fuel required is calculated by multiplying the fuel consumption of the aircraft by the flight time. The flight time will include a reserve to cater for such things as diversion to an alternate airport or encountering a stronger head wind than forecast, the reserve required is dependent upon the type of flight.

The fuel consumption is specified in the flight manual for various power settings and ambient conditions.

The fuel consumption on the outer scale is aligned with the black triangle and against the time taken for the flight, including the reserve, read off the fuel required.

Example.

Fuel consumption   8 US gals per hour.

Flight time   2 hours.

Reserve   40 minutes.

1   Line up the black triangle with 80 on outer scale.

2   Against the flight time plus reserve of 2 hours 40 minutes read off 21.6 US gals on outer scale.

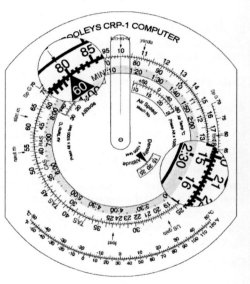

Pressure, Density and True Altitude.

The above three altitudes are defined as:

Pressure altitude is the altitude indicated by the altimeter when the pressure datum is set to 1013.2 mb.

Density altitude is pressure altitude corrected for non ISA temperature and is the altitude at which the current density would be experienced for ISA temperature. Note, ISA is the International Standard Temperature.

True altitude is the measured height above mean sea level and is the elevation shown on a chart.

The computer can be used to calculate density altitude from pressure altitude and temperature. Density altitude is used in some flight manuals to assess the performance of the aircraft.

Density altitude is calculated by using the Air Speed / Mach. No. window, the pressure altitude in the window is aligned with the temperature above the window. Note negative temperatures are to the right of zero and positive to the left. The density altitude is read off inside the Density Altitude window.

Example.

Pressure altitude   10,000 feet.

Temperature   +10⁰C.

1   Align 10 in the Air Speed / Mach. No. window with +10 above.

2   Read off density altitude of just under 12,000 feet in the density altitude window.

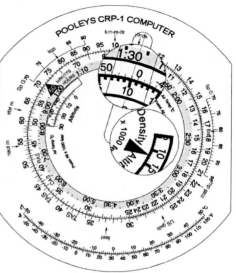

Time En-route and ETA.

The time en-route is found by totalling the times for each leg of the flight. The ETA or estimated time of arrival is found by adding the en-route time to the take-off time. For filing of flight plan purposes departure and arrival times are with respect to UTC. The relationship between UTC, universal co-ordinated time, and local time is discussed in the Time section.

Use of the Wind Computer.

The wind side of the computer consists of a base marked in degrees either side of a reference point indicating drift and variation. An inner rotatable bezel which is marked in degrees around its periphery from 0^0 to 360^0 enclosing a clear plastic window with a blue circle and dot in its centre. A sliding grid, marked with arcs indicating speed and radials indicating drift, which moves up and down within the clear plastic window.

Triangle of Velocities.

The wind computer allows the pilot quickly to solve triangle of velocity problems without having to draw them to scale as discussed earlier.

If we superimpose a scale drawing of a triangle of velocities onto the computer it will simplify the explanation of how it works.

The knowns are, the wind direction and speed which are plotted first, the ground track, direction, which is plotted second, its length is unknown, and finally the true airspeed which is an arc from the end of the wind line to intercept the ground track line.

The arcs on the sliding grid are used in place of a ruler or dividers to represent the lengths of the sides of the triangle and the rotating bezel allows these sides to be represented in the correct direction. The radial lines on the grid allow the angle between the heading and ground track, drift angle, to be easily read off.

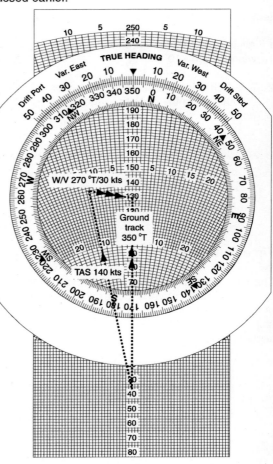

Application of Wind Velocity and TAS to Track.

In a flight planning situation the following are normally known:

Wind velocity.

Ground track.

TAS.

The wind velocity is set first by rotating the bezel until the wind direction appears at the top of the computer against the TRUE HEADING arrow, the wind speed is marked by placing a pencil cross the appropriate distance up from the blue circle. This is simplified if the sliding scale is moved to set a convenient arc under the blue circle, say 100, and the wind speed added to it, so for a wind of 15 knots a cross would be marked at 115.

The ground track is set by rotating the bezel until the ground track appears at the top of the computer against the TRUE HEADING arrow.

The TAS is set by sliding the grid so the appropriate airspeed arc lies under the pencil cross.

Determination of Heading and Ground Speed.

The heading is found by first reading off the wind correction angle, which is the radial over which the pencil cross lies. If this lies to the left of the blue circle the heading equals the ground track minus the wind correction angle but if to the right it is the sum of the ground track and the wind correction angle. The ground speed is found by reading off the speed arc over which the blue circle lies.

Drift and Wind Correction Angle.

Drift refers to the amount the aircraft would be blown off track if the pilot did not compensate for a cross-wind component. The wind correction angle is the opposite of drift and is the amount the pilot has to steer into the wind to compensate for it.

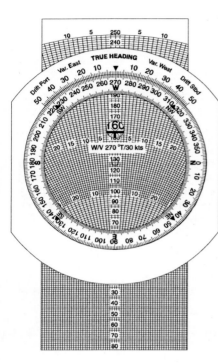

Calculation of Ground Speed and Heading.

By use of the wind computer the ground speed and heading required will be calculated for the following:

Wind   270°T/ 30 kts.

Ground Track   350°T.

TAS   140 kts.

1   The wind direction of 270° is set against the TRUE HEADING arrow at the top of the computer and the 30 kts. is marked by a pencil cross above the blue circle.

2   The ground track of 350° is set against the TRUE HEADING arrow at the top of the computer.

3   The grid is moved until the 140 arc lies under the pencil cross.

4   The wind correction angle of 12° to the left is deducted from the ground track to give a heading of 338°T.

5   The ground speed of 132 kts. is read off in the blue circle.

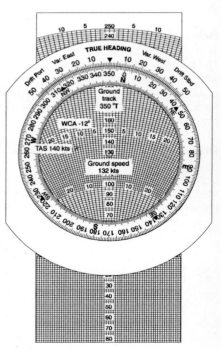

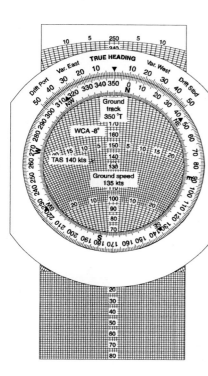

Calculation of the Wind Velocity.

When in flight the pilot adjusts the aircraft's heading to follow the desired track, if this heading is different from that calculated in the planning stage then the wind is different to that forecast.

The pilot is now in a position to calculate the actual wind and then re-compute the headings and ground speeds for the following legs.

For example:

Ground track	350°T.
Heading	342°T.
TAS	140 kts.
Ground speed	135 kts.

1   Set the ground track of 350°T against the TRUE HEADING arrow at the top of the computer.

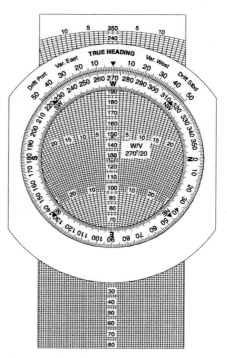

2   Place the blue circle over the ground speed arc of 135 kts.

3   Mark a pencil cross where the wind correction angle of 8° to the left intercepts the TAS arc of 140 kts.

4   Rotate the bezel until the pencil cross is vertically above the blue circle and read off the wind direction of 270°T and a speed of 20 kts.

10

Time.

Relationship between Universal Co-ordinated (Standard) (UTC) Time and Local Mean Time (LMT).

Universal co-ordinated time, UTC, formerly Greenwich mean time, is the standard time reference used for aviation.

Local mean time is based on the start of the day occurring at 0000 hours LMT, this corresponds to the point when the sun is directly over the locations ante meridian. This requires local mean time to vary with longitude which needs a meridian to be chosen as a reference for all the meridians. The chosen meridian being that which passes through Greenwich, hence the old terminology Greenwich mean time or GMT. Due to the Earth's rotation, in a West to East direction, those locations East of Greenwich, i.e. mainland Europe, have LMTs ahead of Greenwich and those to the West lag behind.

Definition of Sunrise and Sunset Times.

Sunrise and sunset are defined as when the top of the sun becomes coincident with the horizon, sunrise obviously is as it is coming up and sunset as it is going down. Sunrise and sunset vary with latitude and time of year, they do not vary with longitude provided the observer's watch is set to local mean time.

The Air Almanac is a publication that provides the relationship between local mean time and UTC for most large cities in the world along with sunrise, sunset and twilight data for most latitudes.

11

Flight Planning.

Selection of Charts.

The charts chosen should cover the route to be flown plus any alternate landing sites and have sufficient coverage either side of the planned track to allow the pilot to deviate to avoid any local weather.

The chart for the en-route phase is usually a current 1:1,000,000, a 1:500,000 or a 1:250,000 aeronautical map, if the flight terminates at an airport then this chart could be used for the approach phase in conjunction with an airport map. Helicopters tend to land at locations away from airports which are found by changing from the aeronautical chart to a more detailed map, such as a 1:125,000 road map, at a convenient point a few miles from the destination.

Route and Aerodrome Weather Forecasts and Reports.

The meteorological service can supply the pilot with various information on the current weather and forecast weather for the route to be flown, this information comes in several different formats.

Most major aerodromes have forecasts produced, called TAFs, indicating the expected weather at the aerodrome for a given time period, usually 9 hours ahead.

Reports of the actual weather at the aerodrome are also available, called METARs, these are taken on the hour and half past the hour, special observations are taken if the weather changes dramatically between standard observations.

Significant weather charts are forecasts of the weather likely to occur over large areas and cover a period of 9 hours ahead, they are revised every 6 hours.

There are several charts issued showing the wind strength and direction at various altitudes, the most common for general aviation use within Europe is the spot wind and temperature chart indicating upper winds and temperatures for spot locations.

The meteorological office requires prior notice to prepare a folder of weather information for a planned flight, in the UK this is 4 hours for a flight of 500 nm or more and 2 hours for less, in Ireland the requirement is 3 hours.

Assessing the Weather Situation.

The departure, destination and alternate aerodromes are likely to have both METARs and TAFs covering the expected time of the flight. The METAR can not only be used to see the current weather but to judge whether the forecast appears correct. If departing from an aerodrome without any reporting facilities it is probable there will be an aerodrome fairly local that will have reporting facilities, these METARs and TAFs will indicate to the pilot the prevailing weather.

The en-route phase of the flight can be assessed from both significant weather charts and, for low level flights, TAFs of aerodromes along the route.

Meteorological Information is available to aircraft in flight on either HF or VHF transmissions, the VHF broadcasts are referred to as VOLMETs. These include plain language reports of the actual weather at local international airports.

SIGMETs are broadcast by ATC on the frequencies appropriate for the areas affected, they are also available when the pilot is obtaining the pre-flight brief. These are reports to all aircraft of meteorological phenomena that may affect the safety of flight, they include:

Lines of thunderstorms.

Severe turbulence.

Severe icing.

Plotting the Route.

The most expeditious route between two points is a straight line but unfortunately in a lot of cases this is not practical due to controlled/restricted airspace and geographical features. This may result in the plotted route having to dog leg to avoid these areas.

On longer legs the drawing of drift lines 5^0 either side of the track originating from both the start and finish of the track will allow the pilot easily to determine any drift due to unforecast winds and make the appropriate correction to the aircraft's heading.

Considerations of Controlled/Regulated Airspace.

Controlled airspace is classified internationally as A through G, where A represents the greatest level of control and G the least. In theory VFR flights are permitted in all classes of airspace except class A, in practice the airspace in the close vicinity of busy international airports may only be available for aircraft taking off or landing at that airport. Even if this is not the case it is probably quicker to route around the control zone or follow any published aircraft routes, to avoid having to hold for aircraft on the approach to or departure from the airport.

If you plan on flying through controlled airspace a clearance is required prior to entering it, in many countries it is mandatory to file a flight plan for all flights entering controlled airspace. Note this flight plan is not a clearance but advises air traffic control of your intentions.

Danger, Prohibited and Restricted Airspace.

Flight is permitted in danger and restricted areas provided the controlling authority approve it over the radio, flight inside prohibited areas is forbidden.

When flying in or in the vicinity of these airspaces a good look out must be maintained since most danger and restricted areas are used by military aircraft either for bombing runs or training. A large number of these areas are only active within given time periods, these periods are promulgated through the controlling countries AIP and NOTAMS.

Use of AIP and NOTAMS.

The Aeronautical Information Publication, AIP, is published by each State and contains aeronautical information of a fixed nature essential to safe air navigation within that State. The contents of each State's AIP follows a standard format, the only variation may be the language in which it is printed.

Notams, notice to airmen, supply information of immediate importance, both short or long term and as forewarning of impending AIP amendments or supplements. Two forms of Notam exist, System Notams, referred to as Class I Notams, which due to the possible urgency of the information are transmitted immediately by the Aeronautical Fixed Telecommunications Network (AFTN) to all major airports. Class II Notams are of a less immediate nature and are sent by post, they advise of future changes affecting aircraft operations.

ATC Liaison Procedures in Controlled/Regulated Airspace.

It is a requirement that ATC issue a clearance before an aircraft enters controlled airspace, this is normally received over the radio following an initial call from the aircraft. This clearance will include a clearance limit, an altitude and possibly the requirement to notify ATC of passing a reporting point. If the clearance is unacceptable to the pilot, i.e. it contravenes a minimum height rule, the pilot can decline it and request an alternative.

Once in controlled airspace a continuous listening watch should be maintained on the designated frequency.

Fuel Considerations.

The fuel required is calculated by multiplying the fuel consumption by the flight time. The flight time must include a reserve to cater for possible diversions and stronger than forecast head winds.

The fuel consumption stated in the flight manual is for a new aircraft and engine, so in the case of an older aircraft this consumption may be a little optimistic. If renting an aircraft ask the operator what its fuel consumption is, weight permitting it is better to take off with too much fuel than not enough.

En-route Safety Altitude(s).

En-route safety altitudes are the MINIMUM altitude the aircraft will descend to for a particular leg of the flight if encountering deteriorating weather. These altitudes guarantee safe terrain and obstruction clearance along the planned route. They are calculated by adding 1,000 feet to the highest ground or obstruction within 5 nm of the planned track.

Alternate Aerodromes.

Alternate aerodromes are selected at the planning stage so if the planned destination's weather deteriorates below the minimums pertaining to the flight the pilot has a suitable landing site. This means for practical purposes the alternate needs to be near the destination but located such that its weather remains suitable for a landing. For example a destination on the coast may experience sea fog whereas an alternate 5 to 10 nm inland may not.

Communications and Radio/Navaid Frequencies.

Communications between aircraft and ground stations should be short and to the point using standard phraseology.

Radio and the VOR navigation frequencies are VHF transmissions and are therefore restricted to line of sight. An increase in altitude will increase the useful range of these ground stations.

Radio and navigation frequencies are promulgated in the AIP, but are also listed on certain aeronautical charts and in commercial flight guides such as AERAD and Jepperson.

Selection of Check Points, Time and Distance Marks.

Check points are used to assess the aircraft's position whereas time and distance marks are used to monitor its progress with respect to its estimated flight time.

Check points need to be chosen with care, they must be distinctive and not likely to be confused with other local features. Typical checkpoints would include several features such as a large town with a motorway crossed by a railway line, or isolated distinct features such as power stations, castles, bridges over rivers even isolated mountains. They must also be clearly visible to the pilot so a town on rising ground may be suitable outbound but on the return flight it could be shielded by the terrain.

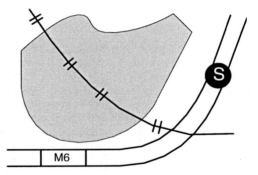

Time marks usually split the leg into 2 or 4 equal portions allowing the pilot easily to revise the estimated time for the particular leg, i.e. at a quarter distance the aircraft is 1 minute ahead of schedule, the ETA can be revised by 4 minutes. Time marks also have the benefit of simplifying any calculations to revise the aircraft's heading if it has experienced drift due to unforecast cross winds.

Distance marks usually split the leg at 10 or 20 nm intervals, again the pilot can revise the ETA accordingly.

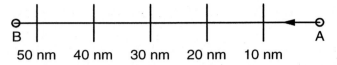

Compilation of the Flight Log.

The flight log sheet contains all the pilot's pre-flight planning for the route to be flown and includes sections to allow for revisions to headings, ground speeds and ETAs due to changes in the winds encountered en-route.

Aeroplane pilots are at an advantage over helicopter pilots in flight due to the hands-off stability of an aeroplane and are therefore able to use their wind computer to calculate new headings, flight times and fuel consumption. The helicopter pilot has both hands full and is only able to make the odd note on the flight log, any calculations are mental arithmetic.

This means different flight logs are required for aeroplane and helicopter flights, but the compilation prior to flight is essentially the same.

A suitable chart is selected and the route is plotted using either a chinagraph pencil on a laminated chart or a soft pencil on an un-laminated one. The route should be as near direct as terrain and controlled and/or restricted airspace permit. The starting and finishing points for each leg are entered in the FROM and TO columns, the true tracks between them are measured using the protractor and entered in the Tr (T) column and the distance between them entered in the Dist column.

The minimum safety altitudes are determined by reference to the terrain and obstructions within 5 nm either side of the track and are entered in the Alt column.

The outside air temperature for the selected cruising level is entered in the Temp box, this temperature and altitude are used to calculate the aircraft's true airspeed which is entered in the TAS column.

The upper wind for the selected cruising level is entered in the W/V box next to the Temp box.

Using the wind computer the true headings and ground speeds can be entered in the HD (T) and GS columns respectively.

Aeroplane Flight Log

Callsign		Date		Enroute Details				

Departure Details

Destination Details

Location	Frequency	QNH	Squark	Weather and other details

		ATIS	APP
ATIS			
TWR	GND	TWR	GND
VOR	NDB	VOR	NDB

QNH		QNH	
RWY	VIS	RWY	VIS
Cloud		Cloud	

RAS	

										Dept Time				GPH			ACTUALS		
From	To	Safety Alt	Alt	Temp	Wind (T) kts	Tr (T)	TAS	WCA	HDG (T)	VAR	HDG (M)	HDG (C)	GS	Dist	Leg Time	Total Time	Leg Fuel	Total Fuel	Leg Time	Total Time	Leg Fuel	Total Fuel

	Est Arrival Time		Reserve
Notes			Fuel Req

46

Helicopter Flight Log

Callsign			Date			Enroute Frequencies			
Departure Details			Destination Details			Station	Freq		
ATIS		QFE	ATIS		QFE				
GND		QNH	GND		QNH				
TWR		W/V	TWR		W/V				
APP		RWY	APP		RWY				
VOR			VOR						
NDB			NDB						
Temp		W/V			VAR		Dept Time		GPH	

From	To	Alt	Tr (T)	TAS	HD (T)	HDG (M)	GS	Dist	Leg Time	Total Time	Leg Fuel	Total Fuel

Notes	Est Arrival Time		Res	
	Fuel Req			

The variation from the chart is entered in the VAR box and then applied to the true headings to give the magnetic headings which are entered in the HDG (M) column.

The flight time for each leg is computed from the ground speed and distance and entered in the Leg Time column, the accumulative flight time to the end of each leg is entered in the Total Time column.

The fuel consumption is entered in the GPH box, this fuel consumption is multiplied by the flight time for each leg to give the fuel required for that leg and entered in the Leg Fuel column, the accumulative fuel required to the end of each leg is entered in the Total Fuel column. The fuel reserve for the flight is entered in the Res box and added to the bottom entry of the Total Fuel column to give the fuel required for the flight. This is entered in the Fuel Req box.

The upper portion of the flight log can now be partially completed, the radio and navigation frequencies for the departure, destination and en-route stations can be found from the AIP, the chart itself or one of the commercially available flight guides. Just prior to take off the departure altimeter setting, wind and active runway can be entered along with the departure time and estimated arrival time.

Compilation of ATC Flight Plan.

A flight plan supplies details of a proposed flight to ATC, flight plans are required for:

Any flight to be provided with ATC service.

Any IFR flight.

Any flight into designated areas or routes.

Any flight across International borders.

Any flight of which 30 nm or more is over water.

These flight plans must be submitted 60 minutes before departure, certain AISs will accept flight plans with a shorter lead time. The flight plan is submitted on a standard ICAO form and can be handed in or faxed into an AIS office. As a last resort certain AISs wil accept it by phone. It is filled in as follows:

The information headed Addressee(s), filing time and originator is left blank. AIS fill this in.

AIRCRAFT IDENTIFICATION. The aircraft call-sign is inserted, G-IBXX.

FLIGHT RULES. Enter I for IFR, V for VFR, Y if IFR followed by VFR or Z if VFR followed by IFR.

TYPE OF FLIGHT. This covers the type of operation, the two applicable to us being G for General Aviation and X for training flights.

NUMBER. This is the number of aircraft, insert 1 unless it is a formation flight.

TYPE OF AIRCRAFT. Insert the ICAO identifier for the type, i.e. C172.

FLIGHT PLAN

PRIORITY   ADDRESSEE(S)

<<=FF

<<=

FILING TIME   ORIGINATOR

SPECIFIC IDENTIFICATION OF ADDRESSEE(S) AND/OR ORIGINATORS

---

3 MESSAGE TYPE   7 AIRCRAFT IDENT   8 FLIGHT RULES   TYPE OF FLIGHT

<<=(FPL   <<=

9 NUMBER   TYPE OF AIRCRAFT   WAKE TURBULENCE CAT   10 EQUIPMENT

13 DEPARTURE AERODROME   TIME

<<=

15 CRUISING SPEED LEVEL   ROUTE

<<=

---

16 DESTINATION   TOTAL EET

AERODROME   HR MIN   ALTN AERODROME   2ND ALTN

<<=

18 OTHER INFORMATION

)<<=

SUPPLEMENTARY INFORMATION (NOT TO BE TRANSMITTED IN FPL MESSAGES)

19 ENDURANCE   PERSONS ON   EMERGENCY RADIO

    HR MIN   BOARD   UHF   VHF   ELBA

-E/   P/   R/ [U] [V] [E]

SURVIVAL EQUIPMENT   JACKETS

    POLAR DESERT SEA JUNGLE   LIGHT FLUORES UHF VHF

[S] / [P] [D] [M] [J]   [J] / [L] [F] [U] [V]

DINGIES

NUMBER CAP. COVER   COLOUR

[D]/   [C]   <<=

AIRCRAFT COLOUR & MARKINGS

A/

REMARKS

N/   <<=

PILOT IN COMMAND

C/   )<<=

FILED BY   ACCEPTED BY   ADDITIONAL INFORMATION

WAKE TURBULENCE CAT.. Insert L for light, M for medium and H for heavy.

EQUIPMENT. Before the / insert the abbreviation for the radio and navigation equipment, S is for standard which includes VHF radio, en-route navigation and approach aids, if no nav. aids and just VHF radio insert V, there are others. After the / insert abbreviation for the transponder, namely: N for none, A for mode A only and C for mode A with altitude reporting. There is reference to mode S transponders but these are unlikely to be fitted to light aircraft in the near future.

DEPARTURE AERODROME. Insert the ICAO identifier, if the aerodrome does not have one or a helicopter is departing from off airport insert ZZZZ and specify in OTHER INFORMATION.

TIME. Insert the planned departure time in UTC, universal co-ordinated time, using the 24 hour clock.

CRUISING SPEED. In our case insert the planned true air speed in knots, using the following notation: N0100 represents 100 knots. Other notations are available for km per hour and Mach No..

LEVEL. Insert the initial cruising level for the flight using the following notation: F090 represents Flight Level 90, 9,000 feet, A050 represents an altitude of 5,000 feet or VFR where no fixed altitude is to be maintained.

ROUTE. Insert the route to be flown. For flights along designated ATS routes use the designator for the ATS route, i.e. G4, then insert each point where a change of, airspeed, altitude, ATS route or flight rules is planned to occur, i.e. CRK. Most VFR flights are on non-ATS routes, insert points along the route not more than 30 minutes apart, also insert points where a change in airspeed, altitude, track or flight rules is planned to occur, between each of these points insert DCT, indicating a direct routing.

DESTINATION AERODROME. Insert the ICAO identifier, if one does not exist insert ZZZZ and specify in OTHER INFORMATION.

TOTAL EET (Estimated En-route Time). This is the estimate in hours and minutes for the flight to the planned destination, it takes into account the forecast winds.

ALTN (Alternate) **AERODROME, 2ND ALT AERODROME.** These are the aerodromes that you specify to use as alternates if your destination aerodrome is unsuitable for landing.

OTHER INFORMATION. This is used to supply other relevant information on the planned flight, for our purposes the pertinent information could include: The departure, destination or alternate aerodromes which do not have ICAO identifiers, these aerodromes are written in after the relevant abbreviation, DEP/, DEST/ or ALTN/, for instance a helicopter departing from Basingstoke would use DEP/BASINGSTOKE. It is not uncommon to miss filling in some of the boxes on the flight plan, if you use the OPR/ term followed by the name of the operator of the aircraft and the phone number it is easy for AIS to contact you and clarify your plan.

The following sections of the flight plan are for search and rescue purposes.

ENDURANCE. Insert the endurance of the aircraft at normal cruise in hours and minutes.

PERSONS ON BOARD. Insert the number of persons on the aircraft including crew.

EMERGENCY RADIO. If you do not have UHF radio cross it out, if you do not have VHF radio cross it out and if you do not have ELBA (Emergency Locator Beacon which if subjected to a sudden shock loading transmits a signal on the emergency frequency of 121.5 MHz) cross it out.

SURVIVAL EQUIPMENT. If you have no survival equipment cross out S, if do have survival equipment indicate the type by crossing out those NOT applicable.

LIFE JACKETS. If you have no life jackets cross out J, if you do have them indicate the features on them by crossing out those features NOT available.

DINGHIES. If you do not have dinghies cross out D, if you have them insert how many and the total capacity, in persons, of all dinghies. If the dinghies are not covered cross out C. Insert the colour of the dinghies.

AIRCRAFT COLOUR AND MARKINGS. Insert the colours of the aircraft and any distinguishing markings.

REMARKS. If no remarks cross out N, or insert any other survival equipment carried.

PILOT IN COMMAND. Insert name of Captain.

FILED BY. Insert your name.

12

Practical Navigation.

This section covers the actual flight, the planning has been completed and the pilot is now in the aircraft.

Compass Heading and use of Deviation Card.

As previously discussed the compass is not only affected by the earth's magnetism but also that of the aircraft. To compensate for any errors caused by the aircraft's structure or electrical components a compass deviation card is installed in the aircraft. This card corrects the indicated compass heading to give the actual magnetic heading of the aircraft.

In practice the pilot applies the deviation to the magnetic heading to give the compass heading. Like variation, an Easterly deviation is deducted and a Westerly deviation is added. This compass heading is then marked on the flight log.

Organisation of In-Flight Workload.

Prior to the planned flight the pilot should have all the relevant charts folded so that the planned track and surrounding areas are clearly visible. These charts should be arranged in the order of usage to avoid having to rummage around to find that illusive chart while trying to fly the aircraft.

The flight log should also be readily available so that progress along the route can be judged against the estimates made in the planning stage. Pencils or pens should be at hand to allow en-route data to be entered on the flight log, this could include actual times and possibly frequencies and transponder codes issued by ATC.

Departure Procedure, Log Entries, Altimeter Setting and Establishing IAS.

The departure procedure will be largely dependent upon local ATC requirements, if possible the pilot will climb on runway heading through 500 feet AGL then turn on course. If the required turn is greater than 90⁰ it is safer to continue in the circuit and turn on course from either completion of crosswind or from downwind, this avoids conflicting with other circuit aircraft.

The flight log entries covering the departure aerodrome may be updated from either the ATIS or ATC if available, and the departure time and estimated arrival time boxes filled in.

The current altimeter settings for the aerodrome are available from either the ATIS or ATC. At an uncontrolled aerodrome they can be approximated by either setting the altimeter to zero for QFE, or setting it to the aerodrome elevation for QNH. Once airborne ATC will provide the current regional QNH.

For VFR flights it is normal practice to use the QNH altimeter setting for terrain clearance yet remain low enough to avoid flight into cloud. On clear days the pilot may choose to fly at a higher altitude in which case the altimeter may be set to 1013 hPa and aircraft flown at flight levels. This will require the pilot to observe the quadrantal or semi-circular rule, (dependent upon the State's Aviation Legislation), which allocates flight levels to magnetic tracks.

Once the aircraft has climbed to its selected cruise altitude or flight level the pilot should select cruising power and allow the aircraft to accelerate to its cruising airspeed whilst maintaining altitude and heading. The engine RPM, manifold pressure and mixture can then be adjusted as per the flight manual to attain the planned IAS and fuel consumption.

Maintenance of Heading and Altitude.

Once in the air the pilot's number one priority is to fly the aircraft. When navigating on a cross country flight map reading, being aware of one's position and progress are additional tasks that must be performed in parallel to controlling the aircraft. The heading and altitude must be maintained to allow the pilot to ascertain any heading and ETA corrections required due to unforecast winds.

Use of Visual Observations.

The prime references for VFR flights are visual observations, these observations may be checkpoints marked on the chart or they may be features that confirm the aircraft's progress. These could be line features running parallel or perpendicular to the required track, such as power lines, railway tracks or rivers. Alternatively the position or shape of rising terrain, or the shape of the coast, can confirm the approximate position of the aircraft.

Establishing Position and Identification of Checkpoints.

The initial checkpoint for each leg should be within about 5 minutes flying time of the start of the leg, this allows the pilot to check whether the planned heading and ETA are correct and if not amend them.

Checkpoints must be positively identified, do not just assume the town below you is the one marked on the chart but check it for the distinct features you noted in the flight planning stage.

Revisions to Heading and ETA.

It is unlikely the winds encountered in flight are exactly as forecast, if this is the case the heading required and resulting ground speed will be different from those planned.

Heading correction can be assessed by using either the one in sixty rule or the closing angle rule.

The one in sixty rule is based on the fact that a $1°$ track error over 60 nm results in the aircraft being 1 nm off track. Therefore each nm off track at 60 nm represents a $1°$ track error, hence if 3 nm off track at 60 nm the track error is $3°$.

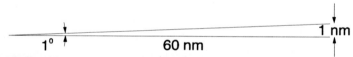

Using this relationship the track error can be calculated if the distance flown and the distance off track are known.

Track Error (degrees) = $\dfrac{60}{\text{Distance Flown}}$ x Distance Off Track

If this formula is solved at the midpoint of the leg then turning the aircraft towards the planned track by double the track error will result in the aircraft rejoining the planned track at the end of the leg.

Obviously it is not always convenient to make the correction at the midpoint of each leg so to allow for the correction to be made at any point along the leg an additional calculation has to be performed. This uses a similar formula to that above but uses the distance to go and results in the closing angle, this is then added to the track error to give the heading alteration required to rejoin the planned track at the end of the leg.

Closing Angle (degrees) = $\dfrac{60}{\text{Distance To Go}}$ x Distance Off Track

For example an aircraft has flown 20 nm of a 60 nm flight and is 1 nm off course.

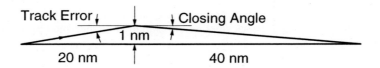

Track Error | Closing Angle

1 nm

20 nm | 40 nm

Track Error $= \dfrac{60}{20} \times 1 = 3^0$.

Closing Angle $= \dfrac{60}{40} \times 1 = 1.5^0$.

Heading Change $= 4.5^0$.

The closing angle rule can also be used to assess the heading change required to rejoin the planned track by making use of drift lines drawn either side of the planned track.

The pilot draws drift lines 5^0 and 10^0 either side of the track originating from the end of the leg allowing an approximation to be made of the closing angle. The proportion of the track flown can be approximated by the pilot splitting the track into a convenient number of equal sectors, typically 4. The heading change required to rejoin the planned track at the end of the leg is found by dividing the closing angle by the proportion of the track flown.

B

15^0
10^0 DRIFT LINES
5^0 15^0
5^0 10^0
10^0 5^0 5^0
15^0 10^0
15^0

Heading Change $= \dfrac{\text{Closing Angle}}{\text{Proportion Of Track Flown}}$

A

For example an aircraft has flown a quarter of the planned leg and approximates a closing angle from the destination drift lines of 5^0.

Heading Change $= \dfrac{5}{(1/4)} = 20^0$.

ETAs, the simplest method of revising the ETA is to split the track evenly into say 4 parts, or another convenient number, On reaching the first split the difference in arrival time multiplied by the number of splits, in our case 4, will result in the change of ETA at the end of the leg.

B   3/4   1/2   1/4   A

Lost Procedure.

A pilot who has been uncertain of the aircraft's position for 20 to 30 minutes is considered lost. This may vary depending upon the terrain, flying over a large residential area such as London or Los Angeles this may reduce to 5 minutes whereas flying across featureless desert it may be nearer 1 hour.

If you become lost, continue to fly the aircraft and do not panic.

Your first consideration is safety:

Are you low on fuel?

Are you running out of daylight?

Is the weather deteriorating?

Is your safety altitude sufficient?

Are you in the vicinity of controlled airspace?

Your second consideration is why am I not where I should be:

Is the directional gyro synchronised with the compass?

Am I flying the correct heading?

Are my in-flight calculations wrong?

Your third consideration is to find out where you are:

Estimate, from your last known fix, where you think you are and draw a circle around this point with a radius of 1/10 th the distance from the last known fix. You are probably within this circle.

Are there any prominent features on the ground that also appear in the circle?

If there are, either estimate a heading to rejoin your planned track, or follow distinct features on the map to return to the planned track, in either case new ETAs will have to be calculated.

If not reconsider the safety factors.

Your fourth consideration is to seek external assistance:

Have you been in communication with Air Traffic Control or a Flight Information Service, earlier, or while uncertain of position, if so can you raise them now?

If you can, state you are lost and need assistance, do not under-estimate your condition.

If your aircraft is fitted with a transponder they will probably give you a distinct code and ask you to press ident, this causes your blip on their radar screen to stand out. They can now give you a position fix and a suggested heading to rejoin your planned route.

If no contact is made make a distress call on the Emergency Frequency 121.5 M Hz. This frequency is continuously monitored by a large number of civil and military ground stations, who should receive and reply to your request for assistance. Since the radio in aircraft transmit in the VHF frequency band it is limited to line of sight, the higher you are, airspace and cloud permitting the better chance you have of being received. Also the emergency services are initially going to assess your position by either interrogating your transponder or by using VHF direction finding (VDF) which takes bearings of your transmissions from different airfields. Since both are line of sight the higher you are the easier it is for them to find you.

If contact is made either through ATC or the emergency frequency the following details will assist the controller to provide you with appropriate instructions to get you back on course or safely on the ground at a local airfield:

Aircraft callsign and type.

I am lost.

My qualifications are............

The weather is VMC or IMC.

My intentions are.............

Approximate position, altitude and heading.

If transponder equipped I am squawking ....

If a call on 121.5 brings no joy and your aircraft is fitted with a transponder set it to 7700, this is the emergency code and if detected by ATC it will set off the alarm bells.

Your fifth consideration is self help, find a line feature and follow it until you reach a large town or other distinct feature you can also find on the map. This final method is only recommended if all else fails since it may lead you into controlled or restricted airspace, or into rising terrain.

Arrival Procedures and ATC Liaison.

When inbound to an uncontrolled airfield, where radio facilities may not exist, the pilot should join overhead at an altitude above that of any possible circuit aircraft. The pilot should report position and intentions even if the airfield appears unmanned, this notifies any other aircraft in the vicinity of your location and intentions. Once overhead the airfield the pilot can view the signal square, if present, to ascertain the active runway and whether any other activities are occurring at the airfield. Not all airfields have signal squares, if this is the case the runway to use will be either that in current use, if other aircraft are in the circuit, or by reference to the wind sock the runway most favouring the surface wind.

The pilot should now position the aircraft so that it is flying parallel to the takeoff direction but on the opposite side of the runway to the downwind leg and, traffic permitting, de-scend to circuit altitude and join the circuit on a crosswind leg.

In the case of a helicopter, which compared to aeroplanes fly at a relatively low level, it is preferred to join the airfield on the opposite side to downwind and remain clear of the aeroplane circuit.

The flight planning stage should include obtaining as much detail about the destination as possible either by reference to State publications or the commercially available airport guides. If neither of these sources cover the particular field ring the owner and get an oral brief and if possible a fax of the airfield, showing runways and noise sensitive areas.

At controlled airfields ATC will advise on the joining method which could be on a long finals or could involve a more tortuous route holding here and there. Radio contact should be made about 10 nm out, this forewarns ATC of your arrival (not all countries require a flight plan to be filed for a flight in certain controlled airspace) which hopefully will allow them to deal expeditiously with your arrival and subsequent landing.

Completion of the Flight Log and Aircraft Log Entries.

As well as flying the aircraft and navigating along the planned route the pilot must not ignore the flight log. The flight log's purpose, apart from supplying all the checkpoints, is as a progress indicator, for example if the head winds encountered are considerably greater than planned the destination airfield could be closed on your arrival, it may get dark before you get there or you could run out of fuel. If close attention is paid to filling in or checking the flight log as the flight progresses the pilot is aware of the aircraft's progress. In the above scenario realising the aircraft is behind schedule the pilot can at an early stage plan a diversion to an alternate nearer airfield.

The helicopter log, although requiring less written input in flight, must also be checked on a regular basis to assess the helicopters progress. Due to their slow cruise speed and limited endurance helicopters are even more susceptible to unforecast head winds and under these conditions it may be more prudent to turn back to the point of departure and wait for a more suitable day.

Radio Navigation Section

13

Ground D/F.

Ground direction finding equipment is not available in all countries.

Application.

Ground direction finding equipment uses the VHF transmissions from an aircraft to give a bearing of that aircraft from a ground station. It is used as an approach procedure or to supply pilots who are lost with a ground position or fix, and a heading to take them to the airfield.

Principles.

The ground station has a directional antenna that receives the aircraft's VHF radio transmissions and presents them to the air traffic controller as a bearing. If two or more ground stations receive the aircraft's transmission a position fix can be obtained by plotting these bearings on a chart.

Since this detection method relies upon the radio transmissions from the aircraft these should be of sufficient length and at regular intervals to allow the air traffic controller initially to get a bearing and then monitor the aircraft's progress.

Presentation and Interpretation.

The aircraft's bearing from the airport, or its bearing to the airport, will be either displayed numerically or will appear as a line on a radar scope.

Coverage.

The State's AIP will list those airports and facilities that have directional finding equipment, the service is usually restricted to VHF radio transmissions only but in certain areas HF will be available.

Due to the transmission being VHF the coverage is restricted to line of sight, the higher the aircraft is the greater the coverage available.

Errors and Accuracy.

The ground station will give an erroneous reading if the signal from the aircraft is reflected by terrain or obstacles before reaching the ground station. The readings also become very inaccurate when the aircraft is overhead the station.

The VHF antenna is designed to operate at its optimum with the aircraft in level flight, if transmissions are made in a steep turn the ground station will receive a poor signal.

The air traffic controller will also, from experience, judge the accuracy of the bearing and transmit this along with the actual bearing.

Class A - $\pm 2^0$.

Class B - $\pm 5^0$.

Class C - $\pm 10^0$.

Factors Affecting Range and Accuracy.

As already stated VHF transmissions are line of sight, therefore to increase the range the aircraft must climb and have no mountainous terrain between itself and the ground station to block the signal.

The ground station will give an erroneous reading if the signal from the aircraft is reflected by terrain or obstacles before reaching the ground station. The readings also become very inaccurate when the aircraft is overhead the station.

The VHF antenna is designed to operate at its optimum with the aircraft in level flight, if transmissions are made in a steep turn the ground station will receive a poor signal.

14

ADF, NDBs and use of the RMI.

Application.

Automatic Direction Finding, more commonly known as the ADF, is a medium frequency navigation aid installed in most light aircraft.

The ground stations are referred to as Non Directional Beacons, NDBs, and are used for en-route navigation and as an approach aid at smaller airports.

The Remote Magnetic Indicator, RMI, is an instrument installed in the aircraft that indicates both the aircraft's magnetic heading and the bearing of NDBs or VORs.

NDBs transmit in the frequency range from 200 kHz to 1750 kHz.

Principles.

An NDB located on the ground transmits a signal of equal strength in all directions, hence the name non directional beacon. The ADF installed in the aircraft receives this signal and by use of a pointer either displays to the pilot the relative bearing of the station or, if an RMI is fitted, the actual magnetic bearing to the station.

Due to the transmissions being in the medium frequency band they are not restricted by line of sight so range is not dependent upon altitude.

Presentation and Interpretation.

The ADF installed in the aircraft consists of three components, the antenna, the control panel and the bearing indicator.

The antenna consists of a combined loop and sense antenna to receive the signal and determine its direction.

The control panel, or receiver, allows the pilot to tune in the required station and identify it. A typical control panel consists of:

Selector switch, this turns the unit on and off, when on either the ANT or ADF position will

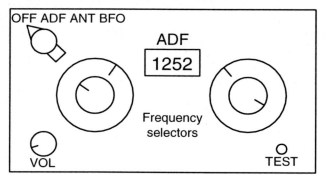

be selected. The ANT position is used for tuning in the station, the ADF pointer on the bearing indicator does not function in this position. Moving the selector to the ADF position allows the bearing indicator to display the relative bearing of the tuned in station.

Frequency selector, this has three or four concentric adjusters allowing each frequency band, (100 kHz, 10 kHz and 1 kHz), to be selected individually.

Tone or BFO switch, this allows certain stations to be identified that are transmitted at a frequency outside the normal hearing range.

Volume control, this allows the pilot to adjust the volume of the Morse code identifier, certain stations will also require the tone or BFO to be on.

Test switch, this checks the function of the pointer. Once the station has been identified and the selector switch set to ADF the bearing indicator should show the relative position of the station. Pressing the test button should cause the needle to deflect away from this indication but on releasing the button the needle should immediately return to its original position.

Once a station has been identified the pilot switches his attention to the bearing indicator or the RMI if installed. In both cases the head of the needle points towards the station and the tail of the needle represents the position of the aircraft relative to the station.

The bearing indicator is surrounded by a bearing card and has a model aeroplane superimposed upon the centre of the glass. The bearing pointer rotates about the centre of the aeroplane and relative bearings are read off against the bearing card. These readings are not relative to true or magnetic North but are relative to the aircraft's heading. To home to a station a pilot would turn so that the head of the needle is pointing at the nose of the model aeroplane or 0° on the bearing card.

The RMI, Remote Magnetic Indicator receives inputs not only from the ADF but also from a slaved compass usually located in the aircraft's wing tip. This instrument therefore indicates the aircraft's magnetic heading, the magnetic heading to the station against the head of the needle and the magnetic bearing from the station against the tail of the needle.

Coverage.

The State's AIP will list the volumes of coverage for each NDB and protection ranges, these ranges are based upon the transmitter's power and the vicinity of other transmitters using the same or similar frequencies.

Errors and Accuracy.

The errors experienced by an ADF are primarily a consequence of operating in the medium frequency band.

At night sky waves form which may, due to reflections, not be coming from the correct direction.

When flying in the vicinity of thunderstorms the pointer will be attracted by the lightning flashes.

Mountainous terrain between the NDB and the aircraft can reflect the signal.

Coast lines can refract the signal, bend it, due to the different energy absorption of land and water.

Other points to watch are that the Morse code identifier is continuously monitored, unlike most other navigation aids the ADF has no "off flag". If using a heading indicator remember to set it regularly against the magnetic compass, a 15^0 heading error will result in a 15^0 bearing error.

Factors Affecting Range and Accuracy.

The range of an NDB is dependent upon the following factors:

Power, the more powerful the transmitter the greater the range, to double an NDBs range requires four times the power.

Frequency, a lower frequency will give a greater range for the same power output.

Surface, greater ranges are available over water than land.

Sky waves, at night the signal from the NDB will not only travel along the ground but will also be reflected by the sky, the ADF is unable to distinguish between the two signals and an erroneous indication results. Sky waves only occur when more than 70 nm from the station, hence at night the range is limited to 70 nm.

Interference, the useful range is restricted by the vicinity of other transmitters operating on similar or the same frequencies. To guarantee that other stations do not interfere with the selected station each State publishes protection ranges in their AIPs.

The accuracy of an NDB/ADF is dependent upon the following:

Sky waves, as discussed above.

Surface, mountains reflecting the signal and coast lines refracting it.

Static, leads to interference and in the case of thunderstorm activity the indications from the bearing indicator can become meaning-less.

15

VOR.

Application.

VHF Omni-Directional Radio Range, VOR, is the most common navigational aid used by all pilots, it gives a direct indication of the pilots angular position to or from the ground-station. VORs are primarily used as the turning points en-route and as the initial approach fix, or even the instrument approach at the destination.

VORs transmit in the range 108 MHz to 117.95 MHz, the lower band up to 112 MHz are normally ILS, Instrument Landing System, frequencies but may be used for short range VORs.

Principles.

The VOR gives bearing information to the pilot by transmitting two separate signals that are out of phase.

The reference and directional signals are arranged so that their phase difference corresponds to the magnetic bearing from the station. The equipment installed in the aircraft detects this phase difference and passes it to the VOR indicator.

Since the VOR is operating in the VHF band usage is limited to line of sight.

Presentation and Interpretation.

The VOR equipment installed in the aircraft consists of three components, the antenna, control panel and VOR indicator.

The antenna is "V" shaped and either mounted on the tail of an aeroplane or under the cabin on a helicopter.

The control panel, or VOR receiver, allows the pilot to tune in and identify the VOR station, a typical control panel consists of the following:

On/off switch, this turns the equipment on and in most cases also acts as the volume control for listening to the station's Morse code identifier.

Frequency selector, this is a double concentric knob allowing the station's frequency to be selected.

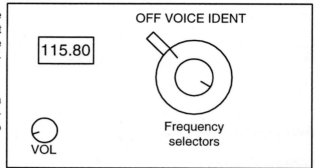

OFF VOICE IDENT

115.80

VOL

Frequency
selectors

The VOR indicator consists of a rotatable course selector, or omni-bearing selector (OBS), which the pilot rotates by use of the course selector knob. The pilot selects the desired course by rotating the course selector knob until the course appears under the course selector at the top of the dial.

A course deviation indicator (CDI) shows whether the aircraft is on course, If so it hangs vertically in the centre of the dial but if the aircraft is off course it moves away from the central position indicating the direction of turn to get back on course.

A "TO-OFF-FROM" indicator is visible to the right of the centre of the dial, this indicates whether the aircraft is flying towards the VOR or away from it. It also has an OFF, NAV or a yellow hatched flag that appears when the signal is either lost or too weak to give an accurate indication.

The VOR is normally used as a tracking aid, the aircraft being flown directly to the VOR or directly away from it on a selected radial. To fly directly to the VOR the pilot turns the course selector knob until the CDI centres and the TO flag appears, the heading to fly is at the top of dial under the course selector. If the FROM flag appears the course you have selected is the reciprocal of what is required, you must continue turning the course selector knob to re-centre the CDI and get the TO flag. Flying this heading under no wind will result in the aircraft flying directly to the VOR but if a wind is present it is likely the aircraft will drift off track, the CDI will alert you to this. If the CDI moves away from the central position it is indicating the aircraft needs to be turned in that direction, so if the CDI moves left the pilot must reduce the aircraft's heading to get back on course. It is recommended the pilot alters heading by 20° in the direction of CDI movement, when the CDI re-centres the aircraft is back on course and the heading correction can be reduced to 10°. If the aircraft remains on course the wind correction angle of 10° is correct but if it is still being blown off course try 15°, similarly if 10° is too much and the CDI moves in the opposite direction try 5°.

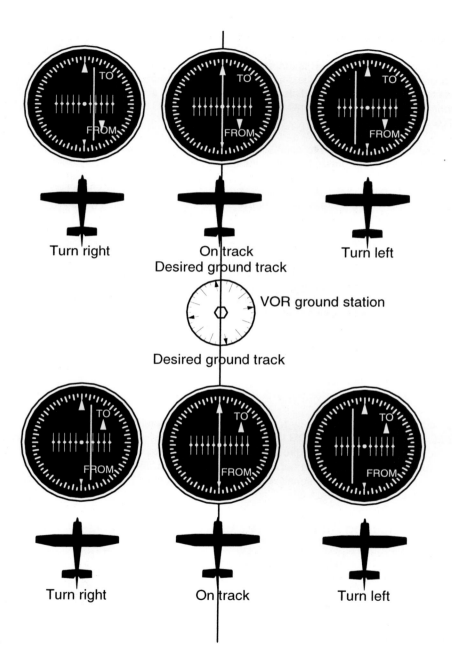

Turn right

On track
Desired ground track

VOR ground station

Desired ground track

Turn right

On track

Turn left

Turn left

On approaching the VOR the CDI will get very fidgety and on passing overhead the VOR the CDI will oscillate from side to side and the TO flag will change to a FROM. If the planned course from the VOR is the same as to it then continue tracking as before, but if the course away from the VOR is different then turn the course selector to the new course. Close to the station the VOR radials are very close together so it is recommended you turn to your flight planned heading until about 5 nm from the VOR then use the CDI to track the selected radial.

The VOR can also be used to establish a fix, in this case select a VOR that is approximately abeam of your present position, tune it in and identify it. Turn the course selector knob until the CDI centres but this time with the FROM flag visible, under the course selector read off the radial from the VOR you are over flying. This can then be plotted on your chart to give you a cross fix of your position, if you were originally tracking another VOR then your exact position is known.

Coverage.

The State's AIP will list the coverage volume, protection range and altitude, for each VOR. Due to operating in the VHF band certain VORs will have sectors that are unusable because to high ground blocking the signal, these sectors will be stated in the AIP.

Errors and Accuracy.

The signal leaving the VOR is accurate to within $\pm 1^0$ and the receiver in the aircraft must be accurate to $\pm 4^0$ for it to be used for IFR flight.

The pilot can introduce errors by trying to use the VOR outside its protection range and altitude, and by setting the FROM flag instead of the TO flag which leads to reverse sensing, the CDI now indicates the direction the aircraft is off track, not the direction to turn to rejoin the radial. As the aircraft approaches the VOR the radials get closer together and the CDI becomes extremely sensitive, the pilot must not chase the CDI but maintain the heading used to track to the VOR.

Factors Affecting Range and Accuracy.

The range of a VOR is dependent upon the following factors:

Power, the greater the power the greater the range, en-route VORs may have a range of up to 200 nm, whereas the lower powered terminal VORs, TVORs, are limited to about 30 nm.

Height, these VHF transmissions are line of sight, therefore the higher the VOR and/or the aircraft the greater the range.

Protection range and altitude, due to the small number of frequencies available for VORs their practical range is normally limited by interference from other VORs transmitting on the same frequency.

Terrain, rising ground between the VOR and the aircraft can reflect, bend or block the signal, leading either to an erroneous indication or none at all. The AIP will include in the protection range and altitude any sectors that are either unreliable or unusable.

The accuracy of a VOR is dependent upon the following:

Location error, the VORs output are ground monitored to an accuracy of $\pm$ 1°.

Aircraft equipment error, for the aircraft to be flown under IFR the aircraft's VOR must be accurate to $\pm$ 4°, this can be checked by using a test VOR or if the aircraft has two VORs by comparing the two.

16

DME.

Application.

Distance Measuring Equipment, DME, measures the slant distance from the aircraft to the DME ground station. Most VOR stations have a co-located DME transmitter that is tuned in when the VOR is selected, this allows the pilot to obtain a fix, as a radial and distance from the one station.

Principles.

The DME in the aircraft sends a UHF transmission to the ground station which transmits a reply to the aircraft. The aircraft's DME records the time difference for the return trip and calculates the slant distance to the ground station. The ground speed and time to the station are also calculated by comparing consecutive time differences.

DME is a UHF transmission and usage is therefore limited to line of sight

Presentation and Interpretation.

The DME equipment installed in the aircraft consists of a shark fin antenna and a display incorporating selector switches.

A typical DME unit has buttons under the display allowing either the distance to, the ground speed to, or the time to the ground station to be indicated, some models display all three simultaneously.

A rotary-three position switch allows the pilot of an aircraft fitted with two VORs to select either of the DMEs associated with the VORs. A central hold function allows the DME frequency to be held when the pilot changes one of the VORs to, say, a station with no associated DME.

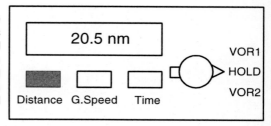

Coverage.

DME like the VOR is line of sight and has a maximum coverage of 200 nm.

Errors and Accuracy.

The equipment is very accurate with an error no greater than 3% or $\pm$ 0.5 nm whichever is greater, most units typically have an accuracy of 0.25% or $\pm$ 0.2 nm.

DME measures the slant distance from the aircraft to the ground station. At high altitudes close to the station errors can arise, when vertically over the station the DME would indicate the aircraft's altitude in nm, i.e. at 36,000 feet this is 6 nm. The difference between slant range and horizontal distance is called the slant range error.

Factors Affecting Range and Accuracy.

Since DME operates in the UHF band its range is restricted by line of sight, the maximum range at altitude is restricted to 200 nm by the power of both the ground and aircraft equipment.

At long distances from the ground station slant range errors are negligible, however closer to the station these errors increase.

17

GPS.

Application.

The Global Positioning System, GPS, is a navigation system utilising 24 satellites orbiting the earth. Aircraft appropriately equipped have a very accurate yet simple means of navigation that locates the aircraft's position and updates it automatically, and gives ETAs, track and ground speed to way-points or destinations.

Principles.

Satellite navigation locates the receiver's, aircraft's, position by measuring its distance from a group of satellites. The distance from one satellite would position the aircraft somewhere on the surface of a sphere surrounding that satellite, the distance from a second satellite would reduce this to the circular intersection of its sphere and that of the first satellite. By measuring the distance from a third satellite the exact position of the aircraft is known. If the altitude of the aircraft is used in the calculation then only two satellites are required. In practice four satellites, or three if the altitude is used, are required to account for any timing errors in the GPS receiver in the aircraft.

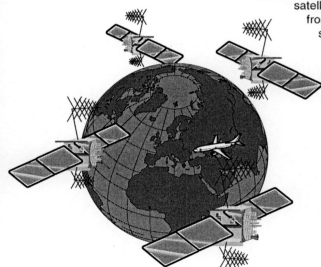

Presentation and Interpretation.

Early GPS receivers had a small screen and only gave the pilot numerical data and maybe an off track indication, the more modern designs have a large screen allowing the graphical display of the route to be flown.

The pilot inputs way-points, these are the turning points, checkpoints and destination, for the route. The GPS then calculates the track and once airborne gives a read-out of the aircraft's track, ground speed and ETA to each way-point.

Coverage.

The coverage is world-wide, the system has even been used in space to locate satellites requiring repair.

Errors and Accuracy.

The GPS is affected by errors present in both the satellites and receiver, but also in passing through the ionosphere and atmosphere.

The largest errors are due to the American Department of Defence degrading the signal by using Selective Availability, S/A, this prevents the "enemy" from having as accurate a navigation system.

Typical receivers will indicate an accuracy to within 20 to 60 metres with S/A off, and with it on to within 120 metres.

Factors Affecting Range and Accuracy.

For the GPS receiver to give a position it requires the signal from four satellites, at the time of writing there are places and times where four satellites are not available, if three are available then 2D navigation is available. When all 24 satellites are in orbit the whole surface of the earth will have four satellites available 24 hours a day.

Early GPS receivers only have a single channel, they monitor the four satellites in series, this can take up to 30 seconds and leads to slight position errors but more importantly it leads to ground speed and hence ETA errors.

18

Ground Radar.

Application.

The word radar is an abbreviation for Radio Detection And Ranging. Ground radar is used by ATC to detect, separate and direct aircraft. There are two systems in use, primary and secondary radar. Primary radar is discussed here and secondary is covered in the Secondary Surveillance Radar section that follows.

Principles.

The ground station transmits a pulse of microwave energy, part of which is reflected back to the ground station by any target in its path. The time difference between the pulse leaving the antenna and it returning is used to compute the distance of the target. By using a rotating antenna not only is the distance known but also the direction, this return is then displayed on a scope.

Presentation and Interpretation.

The reflected energy from the aircraft is displayed as a blip on a cathode ray tube, normally referred to as a radarscope. The radarscope has a beam that rotates about its centre at the same rate as the rotating antenna and when an aircraft is detected it causes the screen to glow brightly as a small blip.

Coverage.

Primary radar typically has a range of approximately 80 nm at 5,000 feet, this range increases with altitude. Approach surveillance radar (RAD) has a range of approximately 40 nm. Precision approach radar (PAR) where available can talk an aircraft down to a decision height of 200 feet.

Errors and Accuracy.

Errors can arise due to ground reflections of either the outgoing or the return signal, this may give a ghost echo of the aircraft nowhere near its actual position.

Heavy rain can reflect radar signals and also block the returning signal, reflected returns from rain appear on the radarscope as clutter.

Since primary radar relies on detecting an object by the strength of the reflected signal, it is possible that small light aircraft may be missed or not picked up until relatively close to the radar station.

Factors Affecting Range and Accuracy.

The range of primary radar is dependent upon:

The power of the transmitter, due to signal having not only to reach the target but also be reflected back, a doubling in range requiring 16 times the power.

The object being detected, the size, shape and material of the object affects the amount of the signal that is reflected back to the ground-based antenna, metal objects are better reflectors than composite.

Rain, a line of heavy showers can block the return signal from the aircraft thereby considerably reducing the radar's range.

Terrain, radar is line of sight hence any intervening high ground will reduce the range at low altitudes.

Altitude, due to the curvature of the earth an aircraft at a higher altitude will be detectable from a greater range.

The accuracy of primary radar is dependent upon:

Ground reflections, these can give erroneous ghost blips on the screen nowhere near the aircraft's actual position.

Primary radar measures the slant distance, therefore errors arise when the aircraft is at a high altitude near the ground station.

19

Secondary Surveillance Radar.

Although primary radar is a simple means of detecting aircraft it has several weaknesses, the most significant being the requirement of high power for long range, that small targets may be missed and the blocking effect of rain. These are overcome by the use of secondary surveillance radar.

Principles.

Secondary surveillance radar employs both a ground and aircraft receiver/transmitter, the ground station sends a signal to the aircraft, which interrogates it and then transmits its own signal to the ground station. By the use of separate transmitters the signal only has to travel one way allowing the use of low power transmitters. The size and shape of the aircraft does not affect the blip on the radar scope as it may in the case of primary radar. The effect of rain is virtually eliminated by the ground and aircraft transmitting on different frequencies.

The aircraft's receiver/transmitter is called a transponder. ATC assigns a distinct code to each aircraft, this appears beside the blip on the radarscope allowing the air traffic controller easily to identify different aircraft.

Application.

Secondary surveillance radar is required for flight in most controlled airspace since each aircraft is identified by the transponder code it has been assigned.

Presentation and Interpretation.

The aircraft transponder has four code windows, an on/off mode selector switch and an ident button. The code assigned by ATC is input in the four windows and the mode selected by twisting the selector switch to the appropriate position, the ident feature causes the blip on ATC's radar screen to intensify for easy recognition.

Modes and Codes.

For the transponder to be identified by ATC it must be switched on and set to a specified mode and code, these are described below.

The mode refers to the position of the mode selector switch:

Standby, the transponder is on but not transmitting.

On, the transponder is receiving and transmitting, there is no altitude information being sent to the ground station, this is referred to as Mode A.

Altitude, the transponder is receiving and transmitting, altitude information is being transmitted to the ground station, this is referred to as Mode C.

Test, the orange reply light should flash indicating the unit is serviceable.

The separate ident button sends a signal to the ground station which intensifies the blip on the radarscope screen.

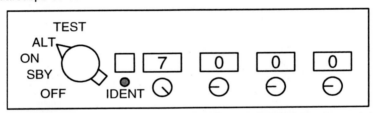

The code refers to the numbers assigned to the four code windows, for certain uncontrolled flights a VFR code is used, in the UK and Ireland this is 7000 whereas in the USA they use 1200. ATC assign an individual code to aircraft by using the term Squawk and the code, i.e. squawk 4321, the pilot acknowledges, turns the transponder to standby sets the code and turns it back to altitude. Certain codes have been assigned world wide for various emergency conditions these are:

7500, indicates to ATC the aircraft has been high-jacked.

7600, indicates to ATC the aircraft's radios have failed.

7700, indicates the aircraft has an emergency.

Index